Communicate Your Way to Success

The Art of Selling Ideas

Table of Contents

Chapter 1. Introduction

In this vibrant and enlightening Special Report titled "Communicate Your Way to Success: The Art of Selling Ideas," we open doors to the realm of effective communication and persuasive selling strategies. The text is pulsing with a lively energy that underscores the essence of sharing ideas, persuading others, and inspiring trust through crafty and strategic communication. Prepare to journey through the vital stages of rapport building, active listening, and powerful presenting. Whether you are an aspiring salesperson, a curious entrepreneur, or just an individual aiming to influence your world more effectively, this comprehensive guide brims with insights that prompt results! Ignite your communicative spark and amplify your persuasive potential. Grab your copy now and ascend towards the pinnacle of success!

Chapter 2. Understanding the Elements of Communication

To navigate the realms of effective communication, it is crucial that we first comprehend its basic elements. In any communiqué, whether verbal or non-verbal, these key components are intrinsically present and understanding them allows us to mould our messages more effectively.

2.1. Elements of Communication

Communication is much more than simply expressing an idea or information. Its multifaceted nature makes it a complex process comprising several integral elements. Let's explore each one of these in detail.

2.2. Sender

The sender is the source of the message or the person who wants to communicate an idea, thought, feeling, or fact to others. Whether you are a manager trying to implement a new workflow, a salesperson persuading a prospective client, or just someone saying hello to a friend, in each scenario, you become the 'sender'. The sender's role involves deciding what to communicate, encoding the message, and deciding the appropriate channel to send the message.

2.3. Receiver

The receiver is the person to whom the message is intended. The receiver can be an individual, a group, or an organization as a whole. The success or failure of communication largely depends on the receiver's understanding, which is influenced by their perception, background, viewpoint, and physical responses.

2.4. Message

The message constitutes the information, idea, emotion, or instruction that the sender wants to convey. It's what flows from the sender to the receiver and is the core of any communication.

2.5. Encoding

Encoding is the process of translating thoughts or ideas into a code or form that can be understood by others. This could be through words, body language, text, visuals, or any other means that best represents the intended message. How well the message is encoded often plays a significant role in how accurately it's interpreted.

2.6. Channel

The channel is the medium used to transmit the message from the sender to the receiver. It could be oral, written, visual, or digital. The choice of channel can significantly influence the effectiveness of the communication.

2.7. Decoding

Decoding is the receiver's process of interpreting the encoded message. Accurate decoding is crucial for effective communication, and it's important to note that it can be impeded by psychological, semantic, or physiological barriers.

2.8. Feedback

Feedback is the response the receiver gives to the sender. It is verification that the message has been received and understood. It could be an answer, a reaction, or even silence.

2.9. Noise

Noise, in communication, refers to any disruption that distorts or obstructs the communication process. It can be physical, like external sounds, or psychological, such as preconceived notions or biases.

2.10. Context

Every communication takes place within a certain context such as physical, social, cultural or psychological environment. It's the circumstances surrounding the communication which could influence its interpretation.

Understanding these elements and their interplay can help us refine our communication strategies. As we delve deeper into each, we would unlock tactics that make our messages more persuasive, our communication clearer, and our influence more significant.

2.11. The Sender: Initiating Effective Communication

The sender is often the catalyst in any communication process. As senders, we have the power to influence and motivate, but to do this we must appreciate some important aspects in our role as the initiator of communication.

The sender's responsibility starts with ensuring the message is clear. The clarity of the desired outcome, whom the message is intended for, why it's being shared, and how it relays the intention, are all essential components that warrant consideration before communication takes place.

Encoding the message thoughtfully requires the sender to bear in mind the receiver's background and perception. If, for example, you are communicating with a non-technical audience, you wouldn't use heavy technical jargon in your message.

This section leads us into a deeper understanding of each element, starting with the sender, which maps the genesis of communication.

2.12. Deciding What To Communicate

As a sender, clarity about what needs to be communicated is paramount. Developing a precise and necessary understanding ensures that your message hits home with the relevance you intended.

Knowing WHAT to communicate is the first vessel in the journey to effective communication. It starts with stripping your message to its bare minimum where the 'fluff' is eradicated, and the core message shines bright.

2.13. Decoding: The Receiver's Craft

Just as encoding is important for a sender, decoding signals is pivotal for the receiver. This is where active listening comes into play. As receivers, when we actively listen, we scrutinize, probe and question until the message is understood as comprehensively as possible.

As we explore decoding, we equip ourselves with the tools not just to listen, but to truly comprehend, and respond capably.

2.14. Noise: Understanding Disruptions

Noise is an inherent part of the communication process. Whether it's the physical noise of a buzzing crowd or psychological noise like preconceived notions, every communication is susceptible to distortions that can whittle down the effectiveness of the message.

Understanding these disruptions and how to minimize or circumnavigate them is crucial to delivering and receiving clear, undistorted messages.

2.15. Feedback: The Communication Full Circle

Feedback is a vital part of communication and completes the communication loop. It's the way the receiver communicates back to the sender, often shedding light on how the message was interpreted. In essence, feedback is a communication about communication, encapsulating the thoughts, feelings or insights from the receiver's end.

Every element has a critical role to play in the grand scheme of communication. By understanding these components, we significantly enhance our capacity to share, persuade, and inspire. This understanding is the first step in our journey to effective communication.

Chapter 3. The Power of Active Listening in Selling Ideas

The power wielded by active listening in interpreting and selling ideas is indubitable. This concept, however, is often overlooked in the pursuit of eloquence and charm. The ability to ideate, innovate, and persuade undoubtedly plays a major role in selling ideas. But it is active listening that fuels these abilities, facilitating a deeper comprehension of client needs and concerns. This chapter aims to elucidate the role of active listening in the sale of ideas and provide practical tips on enhancing your listening skills.

3.1. Understanding Active Listening

Active listening does not simply denote hearing the words spoken by another party. It is a full-fledged process that includes understanding the implications of those words, interpreting the underlying emotions, and forming perceptions based on this understanding. It's an art that involves paying attention to the speaker's body language, tone of voice, and facial expressions, along with their words.

Importantly, active listening also involves expressing this understanding to the speaker— essentially validating their sentiments and giving them an assurance that they are, indeed, being heard. Acknowledging, summarizing, and providing an appropriate response are all elements of effective feedback during active listening.

3.2. The Role of Active Listening in Selling Ideas

Just as a physician needs to understand their patient's symptoms to make a correct diagnosis, professionals striving to sell ideas must comprehend their audience's needs, wants, and problems to offer viable solutions. Active listening provisions the foundation for such understanding. It brings to light the aspirations, concerns, hesitations, and motivations of your audience, allowing you to tailor your idea to their specific circumstances.

Active listening helps build strong, genuine relationships based on trust and validation. By showing your audience that you genuinely care about their needs and perspectives, you create a rapport that can significantly amplify the impact of your idea.

3.3. Practical Guidelines for Active Listening

Knowing the importance of active listening and actually practicing it are two different realms. Here are some guidelines that can help you bridge this gap:

- Maintain Eye Contact: Eye contact signals your full attention and engagement with the listener.

- Nod and Show Affirmation: Non-verbal cues like nodding and smiling show that you're aware and understanding.

- Paraphrase: This involves repeating what you understood in your own words. It helps eliminate misconceptions and confirms your understanding.

- Ask Questions: This demonstrates your active involvement and extracts deeper viewpoints from the speaker.

- Show Empathy: Reflecting on the speaker's emotions fosters a deeper level of understanding and connection.

Practice and conscious effort are essential to master these guidelines. With time, this aspiration transforms into an intuitive facet of your personality.

3.4. Active Listening - Oiling the Engine of Persuasion

Active listening complements and enhances the impact of persuasion by helping understand the right 'buttons' to push and when. The information obtained through active listening serves as the fuel for an effective persuasion strategy. It helps in understanding the underlying reasons behind a person's stance and aids in tailoring a more persuasive argument or idea presentation. It's like reading the user's manual before operating complex machinery.

Active listening does not just add to your argument's validity. It works in reinforcing the trust your audience has in you, ultimately fast-tracking your journey to influence, innovate, and inspire. The art of selling ideas comes alive when it is not merely a monologue but a dialogue - a harmonious symphony of information exchange.

3.5. Conclusion: Transforming Listening into Your Superpower

Active listening can become your secret superpower in the realm of persuasive communicating if nurtured and practiced diligently. It is the bridge that connects comprehension to perspicacity, passiveness to proactivity, and ideas to insightful action. By mastering this skill, you position yourself as an empathetic idea seller—one who understands to influence and listens to innovate.

Learn more, not by speaking, but by practising the powerful art of active listening. Remember, the sky is just the baseline, and with active listening, you are all set to delve into the expansive universe of persuasive communication. Bear in mind that success comes with continuous learning and diligence. So keep practicing, keep listening actively, and witness your persuasive potential reach unimaginable heights.

Chapter 4. Evolving Your Personal Communication Style

In the vast realm of communication and interpersonal interaction, every individual cultivates a unique style that defines the way they resonate with others. To evolve and refine your personal communication style, it is essential to dissect its components, analyze them in depth, and create a deliberate trajectory of improvement.

4.1. Understanding Your Current Style

Before you can proceed with your communication style transformation, you must distinctly identify your existing patterns. Do you typically communicate in a subdued voice, or are you more emotionally expressive? Are your ideas submitted in the format of detailed narratives, or are you averse to superfluous elaboration, favoring a direct and practical approach instead?

Your answers to these questions help in laying out the groundwork for evolution. An introspective analysis of your communication behavior can provide insightful leads about the unconscious influences that presently determine your communication style.

Furthermore, assess the feedback from your surroundings. Recollect instances when your communication garnered distinct reactions. Extract your strengths to cement them in your evolving style and pinpoint areas that need improvement.

4.2. Impact of Emotional Intelligence

The significance of emotional intelligence when refining your personal communication style cannot be overstated. Your ability to recognize, understand, and manage both your emotions and the emotions of others plays a pivotal role in establishing successful interactions.

Active and consistent practice of emotional intelligence in your conversations can transform them from being mundane to being impactful. By being empathetic while addressing others' emotions, you create an enviable comfort space and an engaging aura around your communication style.

To begin with, invest time in honing your self-awareness. Be conscious of your emotions and how they affect your communication. Once you manage to achieve this conscious connectedness, extend the practice to detect and respond to others' emotional states aptly.

4.3. Importance of Verbal and Non-Verbal Elements

While words form the building blocks of your communication, non-verbal signals complete the edifice. Gestures, facial expressions, posture, and tone of voice bear equally important information.

Ambiguity or misconception in communication often arises from inconsistency between verbal and non-verbal elements. Imagine delivering an important pitch with a lackluster voice and slouched posture. It contradicts the seriousness of your words and dilutes the intended message.

Hence, pay equal attention to these non-verbal signals and align them with your verbal communication for achieving maximum impact. Optimizing these aspects ensures coherence and boosts your credibility, creating a more persuasive and confident image.

4.4. Incorporating Active Listening

Active listening rests on the cornerstone of engaging communication. It involves giving undivided attention to the speaker, understanding their perspective, and responding meaningfully. Indicating genuine interest through body language or using verbal signals such as 'yes', 'uh huh', or 'I see' enhances the flow of dialogue.

The practice of active listening fosters deeper connections, allows for clearer comprehension of issues, and reduces instances of conflicts. To seamlessly integrate it into your evolved communication style, be patient. Let the speaker finish before you respond. Avoid unnecessary interruptions, and always mirror comprehension or seek clarification before you proceed.

4.5. Rhetoric and Persuasion Techniques

The ability to persuade is instrumental to selling ideas or influencing opinions. To master this skill, try implementing rhetorical tools and persuasion techniques.

Ethos, pathos, and logos constitute the three cornerstones of Aristotle's rhetorical triangle. Ethos, the ethical appeal, establishes your credibility and trustworthiness. Pathos appeals to the emotions and values of the audience. Logos, the logical appeal, uses reason and evidence to support an argument.

Master these techniques to craft compelling narratives and add an element of persuasive power to your communication. Invoking the right blend of emotional, ethical, and logical appeal imprints your ideas on the listener effectively and makes your communication remarkably impactful.

4.6. Adapting to Different Audiences

No single style fits all communication scenarios. A versatile communicator can effortlessly adapt to different audience types, be it a boardroom setting or a casual conversation with friends. This diversity in style keeps the audience engaged and the conversation relevant.

Identify the emotional and cognitive needs of your audience and adapt your style for best connect. With a corporate audience, lean towards a direct and professional manner, underlining credibility and logic. In contrast, a casual, friendly audience might appreciate a more relaxed, empathetic, and humorous style.

As you evolve your personal communication style, flexibility should underscore its every aspect. The ability to sway between different styles as per situational demands makes your communication style dynamic and influential.

Evolution is a continual process, demanding patient and consistent efforts. As you embark on this journey to upgrade your personal communication style, remember that mistakes and missteps form the stepping stones of learning. With self-awareness, rigorous practice, and mindful application of the techniques highlighted in this chapter, you're well on your way to developing a magnetic and persuasive communication style, bound to propel you towards your success pinnacle.

Chapter 5. Mastering the Art of Persuasion

It's said that persuasion is an art – one that can be mastered. With effective persuasion techniques, you can influence the thinking and actions of others, giving you a significant edge in achieving your goals. Therefore, let's dive right into the detailed discussion of mastering this art.

5.1. Understanding Persuasion

First and foremost, understanding what persuasion is vital. Persuasion is the process of changing an individual's attitude or behavior towards an idea, event, person, or an object through communication. Unlike coercion, persuasion is not about forcing someone to see things your way; it's about presenting your standpoint in an appealing and personable manner, providing convincing reasons for someone to agree with you.

The cornerstone of persuasion lies in empathy, respect, and credibility, and reflects in clear reasoning, compelling evidence, appealing emotions, and assuring your audience of shared benefits.

5.2. The Ethos, Pathos, and Logos of Persuasion

Aristotle introduced three concepts - Ethos, Pathos, and Logos - foundational to the art of persuasion.

1. Ethos is about credibility and ethics. When we recognize someone as reliable and embodying moral integrity, we tend to trust their arguments. Enhancing your ethos requires displaying competence, character, and goodwill.

2. Pathos revolves around appealing to emotions. Emotional appeal can significantly influence decision-making, and effective persuaders stir human emotions to win favor.

3. Logos focuses on logical argument and reasoning. Factual data, statistics, and logical conclusions are instrumental in persuading an analytical, rational audience.

5.3. The Framework of Persuasion

Creating a persuasive argument involves a few critical steps that span research, planning, structuring, and finally, presenting your argument.

1. Understand your audience: Study their preferences, biases, challenges, and motivations. This understanding enables you to appeal to their emotions and align your communication with their perspective.

2. Clarify your objective: Define a clear, attainable goal for your persuasive communication, be it seeking approval for an idea or convincing clients to buy your product.

3. Research thoroughly: Gather accurate and robust information to back your statements. Reliable data enhances your credibility and helps form a solid argument.

4. Structure your argument: Begin with a hook that grabs their attention, followed by your assertion. Present your evidence, discuss objections, and finish with a potent call to action.

5. Deliver with conviction: Informative content alone doesn't persuade; you need to present it with confidence and passion.

5.4. Deploy Persuasive Techniques

There are numerous techniques to increase the persuasive power of your communication.

1. Social proof: People tend to do what others are doing. Using testimonials, reviews, and success stories can effectively instill confidence and persuade others.

2. Reciprocity: Humans are hardwired to return favors. If you help someone, they are more likely to help you in the future.

3. Scarcity: Emphasizing the scarcity of resources or limited time offer can create urgency, compelling quick action.

4. Likeability: Both how you present your message and how people perceive you as a person influence persuasion. Showcase a friendly demeanor, common interests, and genuine compliments to be more likable and persuasive.

5.5. The Role of Non-verbal Communication

In addition to what you say, how you say it plays a crucial role in persuasion. Non-verbal cues like eye contact, body language, facial expressions, and tone of voice can significantly impact your persuasive power.

5.6. Hone Your Negotiation Skills

Negotiation and persuasion often go hand in hand. Well-crafted negotiation skills can smoothen the process of persuasion by facilitating mutual understanding, compromise, and finally agreement.

In essence, mastering the art of persuasion is more than just convincing others. It's about creating a cohesive argument, expressing it persuasively, and ultimately, establishing a connection based on trust, respect, and mutual understanding. This mastery equips you to inspire change, motivate action, and drive success in personal and professional life.

Remember, persuasive abilities are not fixed, but can be developed and enhanced over time. Make it a point to practice these principles regularly, and observe how they're creating a difference in your conversations, in your relationships, and in your capacity to influence others. Embrace the journey!

Chapter 6. Building Strong Rapports: The Foundation of Influence

In any interaction with prospects or clients, rapport represents the runway of your communicative flight. Often misconstrued as the final destination, it is only the take-off point, but indispensable nonetheless. As you set the foundation of your persuasive endeavors, consider rapport as a mutual understanding or a shared perspective that you foster with the listeners. It's the proverbial meeting of the minds that culminates in a harmonious connection, a bond characterized by trust, openness, and goodwill.

6.1. The Importance of Building Rapport

When we lack rapport, we see a disconcerting disconnection brought about by misunderstandings, misinterpretations, and distrust. In contrast, consistent cultivation of rapport fosters a comfortable environment, paving the way for smooth conversations.

Rapport proves instrumental in sales and negotiations, often being the catalyst that transforms an interaction into a transaction. This social tool sharpens your persuasive capacity, unlocking doors that might seem bolted against your ideas or bids.

Let's delve deeper into this critical component of influence and how best to construct it for exceptional results.

6.2. Understanding Human Behavior

Rapport hinges on understanding human behavior. This understanding helps you decipher how people process information, why they react the way they do, and what influences their decision-making process emotionally or psychologically.

Firstly, people generally strive for pleasant social exchanges. Ensure every interaction leaves them feeling better than before. Secondly, people guard their autonomy fiercely. Nudge them towards decisions instead of attempting to force them. Lastly, humans are remarkably reciprocal. Genuine goodwill, respect, and value often find their way back to you.

6.3. Empathetic Interaction: Key to Building Rapport

Empathy remains the cornerstone of rapport. Putting yourself in the shoes of your interlocutor provides a lens through which you see their world. It lends color to their fears, expectations, desires, and views, fostering an understanding that transcends surface-level interaction, thus paving the way for rapport.

To harness empathy, ensure active listening, validate concerns, demonstrate understanding, offer reassurances, and adjust your communication to align with the person's needs.

6.4. Verbal Rapport Building

Verbal communication's power lies not only in the message but also the delivery. To use verbal communication to build rapport, you must be thoughtful and deliberate, employing techniques such as mirror language, the use of inclusive language, and asking open-ended questions.

1. Mirror Language: This simply means using similar words, phrases, or language style as the person with whom you're interacting. It helps make them feel understood and affirmed.

2. Inclusive Language: Using words such as 'we,' 'us,' and 'our' hint at a shared understanding or goal, fostering a communal feeling.

3. Open-Ended Questions: Such inquiries allow the other person to express themselves freely, build a deeper interaction, and show that you value their input.

6.5. Non-Verbal Rapport Building

Non-verbal cues often speak louder than words. People glean meanings from your facial expressions, body language, and gestures—all of which contribute to building or tearing down rapport.

To maximize non-verbal communication, maintain eye contact, nod in understanding, lean in slightly during conversation, and maintain an inviting body language. Match your body language with words to ensure consistency and enhance trust.

6.6. Common Mistakes in Rapport Building

Avoiding common mistakes can greatly enhance your rapport building efforts. Beware of coming across as insincere or manipulative—people can sense these quite easily. Avoid causing offense with inappropriate humor or personal questions. Maintain your focus on the person and be sure not to allow distractions to impair your interaction. Furthermore, act genuinely interested in the conversation and avoid finishing other's sentences.

Leverage this understanding of human interaction to your advantage, observing and practicing these strategies to sculpt and cement the foundation of influence—strong, enduring rapport.

6.7. Review and Practice to Improve

Building rapport comes more naturally to some than to others. However, no matter your starting point, improvement is possible—with continuous review and practice. Each interaction brings an opportunity to learn, grow, and refine your skills. Learning from past mistakes and successful interactions, putting new knowledge to practice, and being patient with yourself will eventually lead to masterful art of rapport-building.

The beauty of rapport lies in its mutual benefit. As you work on effective rapport-building strategies, not only do you stand to gain an edge in your persuasive attempts, your interlocutor at the other end will enjoy enriched interactions. So, let's remember, as we aspire to scale greater heights of success, the foundation of influence—rapport—is vital every step of the way.

Chapter 7. Communication Channels: Making the Most out of Each

Communication channels play a pivotal role in effective transmission of messages. Their selection is strategic, and their usage, an art. If you're looking to enhance your communication skills and make the most out of each channel available to you, you've reached the right place.

7.1. Understanding Communication Channels

Communication channels can be largely classified into three main categories: oral communication channels, written communication channels, and nonverbal communication channels. Each one, holding importance of its own and effective in different situations.

Oral communication channels include in-person interactions, phone calls, video conferencing etc. These channels are effective for problem-solving discussions, immediate feedback, or situations where personal connection is important.

Written communication channels like letters, emails, reports, and texts, on the other hand, provide a permanent record of communication. They allow for thought and precision, and are used frequently in business settings.

Nonverbal channels involve body language, facial expressions, and other visual cues during interactions. Although often overlooked, they contribute significantly to the message's ultimate perception.

7.2. Maximizing Oral Communication Channels

Oral communication channels offer immediate feedback, enabling real-time adjustments to the message or approach. To maximize their effectiveness, a conversational tone is key. It fosters an atmosphere of openness, enabling exchange and understanding of thoughts and ideas.

One excellent strategy is storytelling. Sharing experiences or painting verbal pictures can engage listeners more than mere facts or figures. Remember that your speed, tone, volume, and clarity contribute significantly to your message's success.

Active listening, too, plays a vital role. By mirroring the listener's language and tone, we can establish rapport and encourage a more open dialogue.

7.3. Leveraging Written Communication Channels

In written communication channels, you have the opportunity to craft and polish your message. Nonetheless, remember - brevity is the soul of wit. Be sure to strike a balance between completeness and conciseness, ensuring the receiver doesn't get overwhelmed but understands your message.

Using simple language, avoiding jargon, and using bullet-points or numbered lists allows for the message to be more digestible. Spelling and grammar check should be your final steps before sending the written piece away. First impressions are formed quickly, and mistakes can significantly impact how your recipient perceives you and your message.

7.4. Understanding and Utilizing Nonverbal Communication

Nonverbal cues play a major role in any communication, sometimes even overpowering the spoken or written elements. Maintaining eye contact, using open body language, and modulating your voice's speed and volume can significantly impact your message's interpretation.

Also, don't dismiss the impact of physical appearances. Dress appropriately, maintain a posture that exudes confidence, and always wear a warm, genuine smile.

7.5. Integrating Channels for Maximum Impact

Often, the best strategy is to integrate different communication channels. For instance, complex ideas can be introduced in a face-to-face meeting (oral channel), followed by an email recap (written channel), and ended with an informal chat to answer further queries (combining oral and nonverbal channels).

This integration reinforces the message and makes it easier to understand. And with technological advancements offering more communication tools than ever, options for integration are virtually limitless.

7.6. Conclusion: Flexibility and Adaptivity

While different types of communication channels have their strengths and weaknesses, there is no 'one-size-fits-all' approach. Versatility and adaptation are key to successful communication. Your ability to adjust your style according to the situation, the person you're communicating with, and the message you're conveying, will reflect your mastery in utilizing communication channels effectively.

Master the nuances of each communication channel, leverage their strengths, and circumvent their weaknesses to deliver messages that persuade, impress, and inspire!

Chapter 8. Strategic Storytelling: Unleashing Your Persuasion Superpower

We often underestimate the power of narratives. They serve as a profound element in the art of persuasion, providing a robust base to ignite understanding and breed connection. In this chapter, we delve into the dynamics of strategic storytelling.

=== The Science of Storytelling

Before we delve into the tools and techniques that make a gripping tale, let's understand why stories are so captivating. Stories have been woven into the fabric of our social evolution, serving as the connecting bond between generations, cultures, and civilizations. They invoke emotions, clarify complex ideas, drive behaviors, and impart wisdom.

Scientifically, humans are hardwired for stories. A riveting narrative boosts the production of both Oxytocin, fostering empathy and trust, and Dopamine, ensuring memory retention. Further, with stories, we paint vivid mental pictures that engage more brain regions than facts and figures alone, driving both understanding and recall. When we harness the power of strategic storytelling, we amplify our persuasive potential immeasurably.

=== Building the Base: The Elements of a Powerful Story

Just as a house requires a strong foundation, specific key elements form the bases for a persuasive narrative.

1. A Relatable Protagonist: Against whom your audience can map their experiences or aspirations. The protagonist's journey triggers a psychological phenomenon called 'experience-taking,'

where readers vicariously live and feel through another's experiences.

2. A Genuine Conflict: The conflict arouses curiosity and fuels the narrative. Make it relatable and urgent, placing your audience at the edge of their seats.

3. A Transformative Resolution: Every good story has a resolution that signals growth or change, offering valuable takeaways for the audience.

While a story incorporating these elements can stand tall, the 'strategic' element needs a clear objective aligning with your persuasive agenda.

=== Creating a Strategic Narrative: A Step-by-Step Guide

Now that we understand what makes a story captivating let's walk through the steps to craft a strategic narrative.

1. Identify Your Audience: Your story content, style, and presentation should cater to your audience's needs, interests, and perspective.

2. Determine Your Objective: What action do you want your audience to take after hearing your story? Set a clear, measurable goal.

3. Craft Your Story: Start with a description that immediately sparks interest. Then lead the audience through the conflict and resolution. Make it vivid and engaging, allowing your audience to emotionally connect with the protagonist.

4. Weave in Your Message: The best place to subtly incorporate your persuasive idea is within the story's resolution. The emotional aftermath of a story makes the audience receptive to your suggestion.

5. Practice Your Delivery: Even the most compelling story can fall flat with inadequate delivery. Practice until every pause, and

inflection feels natural and pitch-perfect.

Beyond the Spoken Word: The Role of Non-Verbal Communication

Mastering non-verbal cues can enhance your storytelling impact manifold. These subtle signals can affirm your words, express emotions, and set the narrative's mood. In storytelling, your voice modulation, facial expressions, body language, and gestures play a pivotal role.

During emotionally charged parts of the story, slowing down your speech and lowering your voice can intensify the impact. Similarly, a change in facial expression or a well-timed hand gesture could mark critical story transitions.

Understanding and consciously employing these subtle cues can lend your story an additional layer of dynamism, making it lively, empathetic, and convincingly real.

Finessing the Art: Mastering the Strategy in Your Story

Crafting a strategic narrative is indeed an art form. It marries the engaging essence of a story with the subliminal precision of a well-thought-out strategy.

To give your story a persuasive edge:

1. Involve Your Audience: Incorporate ways to make the audience part of your storytelling journey. This deep involvement heightens their emotional investment.

2. Use Vivid Descriptions: The more vivid your story, the more engaged and captivated your audience will be.

3. Incite Emotion: Positive or negative, stories heavy on emotion stick longer with your audience.

4. Set Up the Aha Moment: Skillfully set up the moment when

everything falls into place. This moment adds a sense of euphoria and helps seal your persuading message strongly.

Strategic storytelling unfolds as a compelling blend of art, science, empathy, and strategy. Master this superpower, and you open a conduit to deep connections, efficient understanding, and impactful persuasion. The art of selling your ideas through stories isn't just about convincing others—it's about triggering action, driving results, and sparking transformation, one narrative at a time! With each tale you tell, may you weave a spell of persuasive enchantment, inspiring others to join you in your ascent towards success!

Chapter 9. Nonverbal Cues: Reading and Projecting

Perhaps you have often heard the phrase "actions speak louder than words". In the sphere of communication, this maxim reflects the critical role of nonverbal cues in conveying messages. It's not only about what people say, it's also about how they say it. The fluent display and accurate perception of nonverbal signals can propel our communicative abilities toward heights of efficacy.

9.1. The Power of Nonverbal Cues

Our biological predisposition allows us to register and understand a variety of nonverbal signals. Every day, consciously or subconsciously, we communicate using these signals. Body language, eye contact, gesticulations, posture, proximity to others, and even our silence, all forms a significant part of the information we transmit.

Esteemed psychologist Albert Mehrabian's studies in communication found that words comprise just 7% of our communication. Tone and inflection play an integral role but remarkably, a whopping 55% of our communication is in the form of nonverbal signals. Thus, it is crucial to navigate these cues carefully, as they have the potential to buoy your message or cause it to sink entirely.

9.2. Understanding Body Language

Body language forms the scaffolding upon which words are held, providing context that words alone cannot deliver. A smile can denote warmth, a furrowed brow might signal confusion, crossed arms could mean disinterest or defensiveness, and excessive nodding could imply nervousness. By understanding these cues, we can work to hone our own body language in ways that support, rather than contradict, the ideas we're trying to communicate.

It is also essential not to focus on a single gesture or posture, but rather the overall pattern, context and clusters of behavior. For instance, crossed arms might not necessarily mean defensiveness if the person is simply cold.

9.3. Power of Proximity

One of the less obvious aspects of nonverbal communication is 'proxemics' or the use of space and distance. These distances can be broken down into four categories:

1. Intimate Distance: It ranges up to 18 inches and is usually used by people who share personal or close relationships.

2. Personal Distance: This ranges from 18 inches to 4 feet and is reserved for conversations among good friends or close work colleagues.

3. Social Distance: Spanning 4 to 12 feet, it is typically used for formal settings and professional acquaintances.

4. Public Distance: Beyond 12 feet, used predominantly for public speaking.

We can manipulate proxemics to influence the kind of rapport and relationships we want to foster. For instance, by maintaining a social distance when in a professional setting, we can help to maintain a sense of formality and respect.

9.4. Mastering Facial Expressions

Our faces are capable of expressing a variety of emotions. Happiness, sadness, surprise, disgust, fear, and anger can all be communicated convincingly and promptly, well before words get the chance to describe them. Mastering facial expressions is an art and involves achieving an alignment between your internal state and the message you want to communicate.

Moreover, facial expressions can function as a double-edged sword. For instance, a sudden display of anger can be effective and might earn respect, but it can also appear aggressive, threatening, and may thus deter people.

9.5. Navigating Vocal Cues

Remember, it's not just about what you say, it's also about how you say it. The tone, pitch, volume, speed and rhythm of your voice, the pauses you make, all add meaning to your message. The same sentence can convey opposing meanings when pronounced differently.

Let's understand this with an example. Saying, "Sure, I'd love to help you with that," in a warm and enthusiastic tone, conveys positivity. However, if pronounced in a dull, monotonous and slow voice, it communicates disinterest and reluctance, notwithstanding the reassuring words.

9.6. Arcane Art of Matching and Mirroring

Matching and mirroring denote subtly reflecting another person's nonverbal cues to ease rapport. By mimicking the other person's behaviors and postures – albeit subtly – we psychologically signal that we are 'like' them, promoting feelings of connectedness and trust.

However, it should be performed thoughtfully. Done incorrectly or obviously, it can lead to more substantial barriers in communication.

9.7. Conclusion: The Road to Fluency

Our journey into the world of nonverbal signals underscores their profound impact on communication. By sharpening our awareness, refining our facial expressions, body language, vocal cues, understanding the power of proximity and mastering the art of matching and mirroring, we can elevate our communicative competency to soaring heights. Remember, the key to successful communication resides not only in clear verbal articulations but also and crucially, in the mastery of nonverbal cues. Harnessing these silent yet potent signals can truly open doors to influence, inspire trust, and sell ideas more effectively.

Chapter 10. Overcoming Communication Barriers

Understanding the obstacles that hinder effective communication is a critical step in crafting strategies that encourage dialogue, foster understanding, and build strong relationships. This voyage through the labyrinth of communication barriers will unravel practical solutions and tactics to navigate challenges skillfully.

10.1. Recognizing Communication Barriers

Before we can overcome communication barriers, it is essential to recognize them. Identifying these stumbling blocks involves being alert to their existence and understanding how they impact interactions. Obstacles to good communication include linguistic and cultural differences, emotional barriers, physical disabilities, and even technological distractions. Be aware of these hurdles and recognize the influence they may exert on your ability to communicate effectively.

10.2. Cultural and Linguistic Barriers

In a globalized world, cross-cultural communication has assumed center-stage. Dealing with cultural and linguistic barriers requires sensitivity, patience, and knowledge. Any mistake in communication can lead to misunderstanding and even conflict.

To navigate cultural differences, learn about other people's cultures, customs, and communication styles. This knowledge will help you to adapt your communication to fit the listener's cultural context.

Linguistic barriers, on the other hand, can be mitigated by employing simple and clear language. Avoid using jargon or colloquial expressions that may confuse the listener. If language limitations persist, consider employing the services of a translator or interpreter.

10.3. Emotional Barriers

Emotions can obscure the path of effective communication. Anger, fear, or resentment can color our perception and reaction to the information delivered.

A useful technique in surmounting emotional barriers is Emotional Intelligence (EI). EI involves understanding one's own and other people's emotions, managing emotional reactions, and using these insights to guide thought and behavior. By leveraging EI, you can control potentially destructive emotional responses, establishing a healthy communication environment.

10.4. Physical Disabilities

Physical disabilities, such as hearing impairment or speech disorders, can present significant communication barriers. However, these challenges can be successfully alleviated through thoughtful consideration and the adoption of supportive communication tools.

For instance, those with hearing impairments may benefit from visual aids or sign language interpreters. Similarly, persons with speech impediments might communicate effectively through written correspondence. Stay patient and adaptable to accommodate these communication needs.

10.5. Technological Distractions

In today's digital world, technology poses its own set of

communication barriers. Constant email notifications, social media alerts, and the seemingly pressing need to respond instantly result in divided attention and impaired communication.

Set communication protocols that prioritize human interaction and meaningful dialogue above the relentless tide of technology. This might mean turning off email alerts during meetings or designating specific times for checking digital messages.

10.6. Interpersonal Skills

Overcoming communication barriers also demands honing interpersonal skills. Active listening, a fundamental component of effective communication, involves fully concentrating on, understanding, responding, and then remembering what is being said.

Nonverbal communication also plays an essential role. Body language, facial expressions, gestures, and tone of voice contribute significantly to the message's overall meaning. Always strive to ensure that your nonverbal cues align with your words to prevent misunderstanding.

Effective communication extends beyond the delivery of messages. It involves the meshing of ideas and opinions, creating a mutual understanding. By recognizing and overcoming communication barriers, we enhance personal and professional relationships, fostering a setting where ideas flourish, and success thrives. Remember, the aim is not just to 'send a message,' but to connect, to understand, and to build an environment of mutual respect and shared objectives.

Chapter 11. Measuring the Impact of Your Communication

The primary goal of communication is to generate a favorable response, trigger action, or effect change. To confirm if your message is achieving its intended goals, it's crucial to measure the impact of your communication. This evaluation entails determining how well your message was received, understood, and transformed into the desired action or behavior change.

11.1. Objectives and Key Performance Indicators

Start off by identifying the specific objectives of each message you send out. Your goals must be clear, measurable, and feasible. Perhaps your purpose is to close a particular number of sales, gain new followers on social media, or convince a client to adopt new software or procedures. After identifying your aspirations, establish Key Performance Indicators (KPIs) to quantitatively evaluate success or progress.

Let's take social media as an example - the KPIs for a campaign could be the number of likes, comments, re-posts, or new followers. In contrast, for a sales pitch, your KPIs may be the number of calls or meetings set up with potential clients, or the amount of sales conversion directly resulting from your presentation.

11.2. Quantitative and Qualitative Analysis

Both quantitative and qualitative evaluations are crucial for an exhaustive communication evaluation.

Quantitative evaluation involves numerical or statistical data. This includes, but is not limited to, email open rates, click-through rates, conversation rate, and sales volume. Tools like Google Analytics, SEMRush, and Mailchimp offer relevant metrics for measuring the impact of various kinds of communication.

On the other hand, qualitative analysis involves understanding the subjective aspects of your communication. Reception of your messages, customers' emotional responses, and changes in perception or attitudes are all evaluated under this category. Surveys, interviews, and focus groups are ideal for collecting such data.

11.3. Feedback: The Direct Communicative Pulse

Feedback is a direct line of understanding to your communicative impact. It's immediate, actionable, and highlights the areas of distinction, while shedding light on parts that require improvement.

Feedback takes various forms, including verbal praise or criticism, written evaluations, online reviews, survey responses, or even facial expressions and body language during a face-to-face interaction.

11.4. Adapting for Enhanced Results

Evaluation means little without action. Once you have your feedback and evaluation results, adapt your strategy to enhance future results. Re-evaluate your communication strategy, content, format, or channel based on your findings. Always be open to refining your approach. The essence of effective communication lies in its dynamic nature.

For instance, if your social media metrics reveal that your posts generate more interactions over the weekends, adjust your posting schedule accordingly.

11.5. Measuring Over Time

Effective communication is not a one-time event but a continuous process. It's essential, therefore, to measure the impact of your communication over time. This comprehensive evaluation will reveal patterns and trends, helping you understand if your message sustains interest and yields the desired outcomes over the long haul.

Measuring the impact of your communication allows you not only to understand the overall influence of your messages but also to fine-tune your approach, leading to improved results in the future. The ability to persuasively and strategically share ideas is potent; through careful evaluation and adaptation, this power becomes a catalyst for tangible success. Whether your goal is to gain new sales, shift perceptions, or merely persuade others more effectively, never underestimate the importance of measuring your effect. After all, in the words of management guru Peter Drucker, "What gets measured gets improved."